How Old Are You?

Gbenga Odunlami

Gbenga Odunlami

ISBN: 978-978-981-588-3

www.gbengaodunlamisignatures.com

Published by:
Daneliherald Communications (Print Doctor Africa)
www.printdoctorafrica.com

All Bible quotations are taken from the New King James version except otherwise stated for emphasis.

This Book Is a Gift from

____

To

____

On the Occasion Of

____

TABLE OF CONTENTS

Acknowledgements

I am extremely grateful to God, my One and only Eternal Best

To the year 2006/2007 members of TACSFON OOUTH / Ikenne who got so blessed by the message I preached on the same title in our last Sunday service for the Year 2006. It was burning, blazing and it is still fresh.

I thank all members of Light Breeds Assembly who have been taught some of the things shared in this book. I appreciate your belief in me and the mandate. May God honour you.

Many thanks to the Odunlami family, especially my deceased dad (Pa J. B Odunlami, JP), whose passion for buying and reading books was contagious. My brother, Segun Odunlami, for opening up his library to me for study those years we lived together. To all my friends - elderly and younger friends--whose successes inspire me to keep moving. Mentors and teachers around the world whose books, messages, personal contacts and lives have caused me to grow, especially my father in the Lord, Reverend Yemi Graceman Aduloju and my precious mentor, TPL. Toyin Ayinde, who wrote the foreword of this book despite his busy schedule when he was the commissioner in Lagos State some years ago.

I am eternally grateful to Reverend Sam and Pastor Nike Adeyemi for giving to the Lord. Daystar Christian Centre is not just a church; it is a maternity centre for destinies and a mountain for radical transformation.

To Mr and Mrs Adeyemi who did the first editing of this book. I appreciate your concerted effort at seeing that it is worth being called a masterpiece.

To my precious wife and sweetheart, Abiola, for believing in me when we met then, now that we are together and forever. To my beautiful children, I am blessed living my life with you.

To my publishing team at Print Doctor Africa Ltd, led by Ayodeji Ebadan, thank you very much

DEDICATION

To the Almighty God.

Gbenga Odunlami

FOREWORD

How do life and time relate? Life is indeed about time and time is measured in season. Every man born on earth is subject to the seasons of life.

With the coming and going of seasons, man measures his time on earth, which he calls age. As man advances in age, he naturally tries to measure his achievements with his length of time on earth (age). This brings to mind the fact that a life lived without purpose is meaningless.

In our clime, there seems to be standards set for some pedestals in life with a particular age. Thus, age becomes a factor in measuring certain achievements. For those who seem to have met the standard there is the courage to mention or reveal their true age, while those who have fallen short of societal expectation would rather conceal their true age.

It is appointed that life is meaningless if it is not measurable with accomplishment. So, age gives an indication of how long we have stayed, and knowing that we cannot live forever, we are concerned about what we have achieved at a particular age. Perhaps more important than age is another factor to life - "principles", the laws that govern life. When principles are followed rightly, the result is excellent living.

In this book, Gbenga says there is hope. You can always have a second chance if you missed your way. It is therefore an opportunity to reflect on the past, and to be assured that the future can be better than the past if we make up our mind to get back on track. What a great relief!

We don't have to end the journey badly after all.

I wish to commend this book to all who have a purpose to fulfil in life.

Welcome to a better life.

Olutoyin Ayinde

Lagos State Commissioner for Physical Planning and Urban Development (2011-2015).

INTRODUCTION

"7 Then Joseph brought in his father Jacob and set him before Pharaoh: and Jacob blessed Pharaoh, 8 Pharaoh said unto Jacob, "How old are you?" Gen. 47:7-8 (NKJV).

Reading this portion of Scriptures, what got my attention was the fact that King Pharaoh had never seen Jacob before and had not said anything to him except this first statement: the question about how he had spent his lifetime. The first word I expected him to utter should revolve around appreciating him for bringing Jacob who had earlier pronounced blessing on him before any other thing; rather, the Egyptian king showed much concerned about how this old man had spent his lifetime. I have never seen that particular question in the Bible. It is a soul-searching question one needs to ask oneself to know how one is doing and do something reasonable with time. We should not wait to be asked. We should ask ourselves now.

"Accept the responsibility for the past failures on our part"

That being said, it is amazing that people love to keep their age as a secret or raised for ego's sake in this part of the world. It is only failures that do that because if you are successful and your successes are reasonably at par with the time spent in this life, you will definitely be confident to tell people your true age. On the other hand, people who declare raised age do not actually want other people to be looking down on them. So, they start claiming a raised age for the fear of being regarded as inferior. Surprisingly, they reduce it when there is an opportunity for people in the age bracket below theirs. For example, someone who is 39 years old claiming that he is 27 because of a job opening or business opportunity that has the lower age as a requirement. This act in itself is a poverty and scarcity mentality which puts question mark on their integrity.

Hence, we are to focus on the good use of our lifetime, accept the responsibility for the past failures on our part and for not using the time judiciously and move on with life by doing better in every given opportunity.

Section 1: Time

Gbenga Odunlami

1

Age Is Time

"Teach us to count every passing day till our heart finds wisdom"
- Psalm 90:12 (Knox Translation).
"Teach us, then, how to interpret our existence so that we may acquire a discerning mind"
- Psalm 90:12 (Harrison Translation).
"Teach us to order our days rightly that we may enter the gate of wisdom"
- Psalm 90:12 (New English Bible).

60 seconds make 1 minute.

60 minutes make 1 hour.

24 hours make 1 day.

7 days make 1 week.

4 weeks make 1 month.

12 months make 1 year.

We can see how important time is to our success or failure in life. The tomorrow you talked about yesterday is today and the next year you talked about last year is this year. You have no excuse again because today is a seed of opportunity in your hand to be planted wisely for a beautiful tomorrow. Nobody becomes or achieves anything today without properly planning for it yesterday. Remember, the power of execution and implementation lies with you. You can see thousands of minutes wasted in the past years, but thank God for His mercy which calls for repentance (a U-turn in our thinking and action). After some thousands of minutes, we say someone is a year older without really acknowledging what they have achieved during the period. Only fools doubt proof, and it is not how far but how well. Maturity is not a function of age, but the fruit to show with respect to time. On the threshold of every new year for individuals (birthday) and for everybody (the global New Year in January), there should be a plan on how to maximize those thousands of minutes in the year productively to achieve God's purpose for our lives.

You need to make a decision to make every minute count and live life purposefully by sincerely answering why you are doing what you are doing. This is because time is the currency that God has given us on this side of eternity to trade with. Until purpose is defined, its abuse, misuse, under-use or non-use is inevitable. Even sleeping should be purposeful i. e. for restoration and renewal of strength and health. Today, many people cannot delay the gratification or craving for sleep. I have observed that it is not the number of hours that you spend sleeping that count but how purposeful you are and the mind-set with which you embark on the rest. Eating is not only for pleasure but also for health. Maturity is the ability to delay gratification i. e. self-control, patience and staying ability. Control your desires. Do not allow them to control you. Many people embark on trips without making the most of them. Some spend the time sleeping, Some spend it chit-chatting, Some, reading, while some keep pressing phones. Some wait at office receptions doing nothing but sleeping carelessly, wasting some of the precious tens of minutes there.

> *"Money is a medium of exchange of value, time is also a means of exchange of value"*

A great General of Faith and an Apostle of prayer in Nigeria, Dr. D. K. Olukoya, once made a statement I consider to be very true:, "When you are less busy and there is no work for you to do, do not waste that time for unproductive activities, just use that time to pray even if it is not your prayer time. The time you spend communicating with God has worth more than money or time itself."'. We are stewards of time, as 1st Corinthians 4:2 confirms: ***"Moreover, it is required in stewards that one be found faithful."***

"Time is very transactionary" Time is an indispensable resource that needs to be well-managed. Time management should evolve as a management course. We have heard of Business Management, Project Management, Human Resources Management, etc. Though time management is part of these, it is essential that we major in it. It is important in business meeting management. 2 hours meeting should be 2 hours. Though it requires some level of discipline and management skill to reach this level, it is important because people will respect you for it. For instance, when you are managing the time of a meeting, you need to determine the purpose of the meeting, which must be well defined, clearly spelt out, clearly written and communicated via the meeting notice sent to the participants, including agenda which is strictly related to the purpose statement of the meeting. You must guard against any contribution or input that may change the discussion or meeting flow from the purpose of gathering or meeting. You of all people know that anything unrelated to the purpose of the meeting is a time waster. Urgent and pressing issues can be discussed after the meeting or after the purpose for that meeting has been achieved and there is still some time. Time limit should also be predetermined before any meeting to guard against anything that may waste time unnecessarily. During participation and contribution, set time limit for each person's contribution to the discussion and establish ground rules. For example, if you have talked before, you should not talk again. Except everybody has talked and there is still time, do not interrupt when someone else is talking and some other meeting disciplinary measures.

In church, many young minds leave most of the old churches because they feel they waste the time they are supposed to spend on other activities. Remembers, we will give account of how we spend the time given to us by God as a seed and capital base to do business with, as it is money in an intangible form. Like idea, it has value. Time is a means of exchanging value like money also is. When you invest time acquiring and mastering a skill, you will sooner or later attract the material and monetary equivalence.

Time is highly transactional that we must make a wise use of. I like Ephesians Chapter 5 and verse number 16 which reads: ***"Redeeming the time because the days are evil."*** However, if you examine the 15th and 17th verses respectively, you will see how remarkable and instructive they are: ***"See then that you walk circumspectly (thoughtfully and strategically) not as fools but as wise"*** and ***"Wherefore be ye not unwise, but understanding what the will of the Lord is."*** The Amplified translation of the two verses reads: ***"Live carefully then how you walk! Live purposefully, worthily and accurately, not as the unwise and witless, but as wise (sensible, intelligent person)*** and ***"Therefore do not be unwise, but understand what the will of the Lord is."***

Examine the phrase **"redeeming the time"** closely. The word **"redeeming"**, in the Strong's Exhaustive Concordance of the Bible, has a Greek equivalence **"exagorazo"**, which means **"to buy up, rescue from loss, and improve opportunity."** This shows exactly how to spend time. We are to avoid loss time or downtime. Don't be lagging and lazy in discharging your duties. Learn to say no to distractions. Until you say no, you will continue to live a low life. You can determine when to take a siesta and meal, not the other way round. You and God are in the control room of your desires. Your life and organisation should be progressive year in year out. Do everything you can to get what God is doing and will be doing through you per time because His will always moves us forward. Be 100% committed to whatever you set out to achieve. If you know you can't fully concentrate on it, don't move close to it.

We all need to gain mastery over time and master the art of time management as one-minute loss is very critical to destiny. We must learn how to do the right thing per time by prioritising our tasks. To date, many people still do not understand and use Pareto 80/20 principle in their daily life's time management. It is amazing that some of these people are managers of huge businesses. If you, in particular, have yet to know about it, it is right here, explained in the least understandable manner: spending 80% of your time with the top 20% people in your life that will give you 80% of your result or spending 80% of your time on the top 20% of your task or activity that will give you 80% of your result. Dwight D. Eisenhower, the 34th President of the United States, said, "What is important is seldom urgent and what is urgent is seldom important." This statement was the basis for his prioritising criteria which he stated as thus: "Tasks that are unimportant and not urgent should be done later, deleted, or delegated, while tasks that are important and not urgent should be given a high priority, scheduled, and not delegated".

Karen Leland and Keith Bailey in their book "Time Management in an Instant", clarified the difference between urgent and important tasks, saying: "Urgent tasks are those tasks that require immediate action and attention, while important tasks are those tasks that move you closer to your goal(s)". There are tasks that are urgent but not goal-oriented. Some are goal-oriented but not urgent, while some are both urgent and goal-oriented. Thus, on a daily basis, we should know what to do, what to dump, delete and discard, what to defer or postpone to a set and defined time and date and what to delegate. Some organisations are just counting years with nothing to show for it. I know of a manager who always asks his people at the close of working hour this question: "What value have you added to this business today?"

For me, the question is reasonable because business is about value. It reminds me of a big signage at the exit gate of the secondary school I attended with the bold inscription "What have you achieved today?" As a business owner and business partner, you need to ask yourself how your business is faring year in year out as you must have something to show for it. Lack of growth of an organization sometimes may not be the fault of the visionary but his people. The Scripture says, "Without vision, people perish." Vision also perishes without people. There are members of staff of organisations that are not fully committed to the vision. Like the proverbial servant who buried his talent, some team members may think that the visionary is just using them to fulfil his own desires. That is the rebel's mentality. Every team leader must identify these unfaithful and rebellious people on their team. A wise man once said, "I will rather work with someone who is not able but faithful than work with a rebel who is able but not faithful."

Dear Esteemed Reader, there is a way faithfulness enhances ability. Examining the way Apostle Paul, under the powerful influence of the Holy Spirit, wrote about faithfulness and ability will make you realise that it is faithfulness first before ability; and that building character before competence is very good. In 2nd Timothy 2:2, he said. ***"And the things that you have heard from me among many witnesses, commit these to FAITHFUL men who will be able to teach others also."***

Some people's spiritual life keeps going down the drain every time. They keep numbering the years they got born again and years they have spent in a church. The questions that readily come to mind are: What do they have to show for the years? How are they growing up spiritually? Are they fulfilling their personal ministries? Have they discovered their individual calling and role in the body of Christ? How many souls have they won to the kingdom of God? How is their character, the fruit of the spirit? This and many other questions need to be answered to really know how well we are doing. As the popular maxim says, "It is not how far but how well." It is not about being 40 years old: neither is it about our ministry that is 7 years old. The tangible impacts made, lives touched etc. are the vital signs of how well we are doing.

2

Understanding the Times

"...the fastest runner does not always win the race, and the strongest does not always win the battle, the wise sometimes go hungry, and the skilful are not necessarily wealthy, and those who are educated do not always lead successful lives. It is all decided by chance, BY BEING IN THE RIGHT PLACE AT THE RIGHT TIME **(Ecclesiastes 9:11, New Living Translation).**

"To everything there is a season, a time for every purpose under heaven"
(Ecclesiastes 3:1).

"He has made everything beautiful in its time"
(Ecclesiastes 3:11).

"Of the sons of Issachar who had understanding of the times, to know what Israel ought to do"
(1 Chronicle 12:32).

There is a time dimension to every life's activity and endeavour, as God, in His infinite wisdom and power, designed life to be. That is why it is very important to know God's timing as we discern and discover His purpose for our lives. Let's get the best out of different Bible translations of Ecclesiastes 3:11.

"He has made everything to suit its time- The New English Bible.

"All that He does is apt for its time- The Jerusalem Bible.

"He has made everything right in its time- The Bible in Basic English.

"He assigned each to its proper time"- Moffatt Translation.

Let us check that of Ecclesiastes 3: 1

"Time is for all things but there is a particular portion of time for every particular affair under heaven"- Septuagint

"For everything there is a fixed time, and a time for every business under the Sun"- The Bible in Basic English.

"For everything there is an appointed season and there is a proper time for every project under heaven"- Berkeley Version in Modern English.

"Everything has its appointed hour; there is a time for all things under heaven"- Moffatt Translation

"There is a time dimension to every life's activity"

We need to know what time is and maximise each season of our lives because there are seasons in life. The truth is, seasons don't last forever.

As one who understood times and seasons, Joseph saved the surplus food they had in Egypt for the season of scarcity. I know that we never want bad times, but we need to anticipate times of greater responsibilities and commitments which demand more resources from us. As we prepare for that time, we need to understand that our waiting time should be the time to load, learn, develop and build capacities through training. Every change of status requires a change of skill, knowledge and attitude.

The skill set of a technician is different from a manager's and an executive's in an industry. I have learnt that preparedness always precedes opportunity; it is the proof of foresight. My pastor, Reverend Sam Adeyemi, once said, "When you are trying to be ready when you are supposed to have been ready, you are already late."

Yes, opportunity will definitely come. But how prepared are you to fit into it. God does not put oversized garments of blessing on people; neither can new wine be poured into an old wine skin. *"Go and make your valley full of ditches and the Lord will fill it up with rain"* is the instruction in 2 Kings 3:16. While it is God's responsibility to fill ditches up with rain, it is man's responsibility to prepare the valley with ditches for the rain.

"We need to know our waiting time, it should not be our wasting time but should be our loading time, learning time, time for next level's capacity development"

When you overstay your welcome in a phase or level in life due to your inaction and complacency, you become stinking and deteriorating. Conversely, when you outgrow a phase due to capacity development and skills acquisition, you show the readiness for something big awaiting you at the other end.

Before I conclude this subject, it is important for you to know that our life is like an Automated Machine designed or programmed to undergo a SEQUENCE of activities and phases within a period of time during which things happen by themselves functionally without any stress. Therefore, you need the wisdom to know what time it is and what you should be doing per time.

There was a time in my life that I had all the time to do whatever I wanted to do, as I was not on a full-time job. I maximised the season to read books voraciously. I will forever appreciate the knowledge seeds sown into my destiny then. Those seeds have grown now, with their strong roots spreading everywhere and manifesting their eternal prowess.

When you walk with God, you will always have a revelation of what to do and where to be per time. Though it may be against popular opinion, dare to follow God's directives. Yield to His plan and His Spirit's leading. I love what Galatians 5:25 says in the New Living Translation: ***"Since we are living by the Spirit, let us follow the Spirit's leading in every part of our lives."***

3

Yesterday, Today and Tomorrow
Creating a Future

"Until the desire to go forward becomes greater than the memories of the past pain, you will never possess the power to create again"

- Archbishop Benson Idahosa

Do not dwell on yesterday. It is gone for good. Kay Lyons Stockham once said, "Yesterday is a cancelled check; tomorrow is a promissory note; today is the only cash you have- so spend it wisely." The way you spend today determines a whole lot how tomorrow will be. The pains and regret of inaction or wrong deeds may hurt you. Complacency or pitching tent with the little success of yesterday will want to draw us back, but we are not to live in it. Even the Scripture tells us in Isaiah 43 verses 18-19 that: ***"Remember not the former things, neither consider the things of old, behold I will do a new thing now it shall spring forth."*** Paul also, in his letter of admonition to Philippian believers wrote: ***"... but this one thing I do, forgetting those things which are behind and reaching forth unto those things which are before"*** (Philippians 3:13). Sometimes, it may not be easy to forget the past and look forward. It takes a deliberate and conscious effort to do that.

> ***"Those who refuse to let the past pass away, in no time will pass away with the past"***

Dear Esteemed Reader, God has already forgiven you. Forgive yourself. Never allow your past mistakes to take pre-eminence over your feelings and destiny. Let go of the past. Though you can learn some lessons from the failure or success of the past, try to undo or outdo (if it is success) and unlearn the past. Better days —for which God reserves the best--are ahead. Those who do not let go of their past will pass away with the past in no time. Do not bask in your former glory. Be upward, forward and onward in your thinking and action. Get ahead for the new glory. Our God is a God of the NOW. He is I AM that I AM!

In Hebrews 11:1, "now" leads the pack: ***"now faith is…"*** This is the same as 1 John 3:2 that reads: ***"now are we the sons of God (not will be)."*** When God spoke to Adam, He said*: **"Where are you?"*** God relates with us with our today. God does not have a past; neither does He recognise it. The past is always gone with God. That is why when He blots out our transgressions, it is forever forgotten in His record. You may be amazed when you tell Him how bad you were in the past and He tells you He does not know about it or remember it; hence, it is a forgotten issue. Nobody wants to know how brilliant or intelligent you were in your primary school. They want to know how well you are doing now. I will encourage you to live your best today by burying the fears of yesterday.

It is what we do today that determines our tomorrow. Therefore, today is the springboard for tomorrow. God does not say that we should not plan for tomorrow. He says we should not worry or be anxious about it, putting ourselves under undue pressure in the process. In Proverbs 23:18, the Bible talks about the future: ***"There is a future (a version reads, surely there is an end) and the expectation of the righteous shall not be cut off."*** Therefore, we need to have expectations for the future. It is not late to make any change if your yesterday was bad; it is left for you to create your tomorrow with the judicious use of today.

Nothing changes as long as you hold on to the past. Do not wait for things to happen. Make things happen. Appreciate God for the past, now and the future. Never worry. There is no amount of worry that will make God to do today what He intends to do tomorrow. Worry, complaint and grumbling will not make anything good happen. Just relax. Do not be like the children of Israel who staggered at faith through unbelief, murmur and rebelliousness, thereby elongating the duration of their sojourn in the wilderness.

"...nobody will mind you until you mind your mind"

You may not be where you want to be, but thank God you are not where you used to be. Also, appreciate God for where you are now because everything you thank God for will always multiply. Forget how bad the circumstances that surrounded your birth were or how your growing up was. I told you before that you should let go of the past. When you begin to brood over or meditate on it, you may be drawn back to the mess.

Hebrew 11:15 reads: ***"… if they had been mindful of that country from whence they came out, they might have had opportunity to have returned."*** Dear Esteemed Reader, look forward and upward. Do not let your past determine your future, not the other way round. Make up your mind to sit with the princes, not only to stand before kings but also to wine and dine them. Success is not a product of chances but of choices. The choices we make will in turn always make or break us. Be intentional and deliberate, having discovered who God made you to be and what He created you to do.

Creating the Future

The first time my pastor said the future is created, the Holy Spirit started explaining to me how profound it is. Corroborating this is what the King James' version of Hebrew 11:3 says: ***"through Faith we understand that the worlds were framed by the Word of God."*** Philips translation explicitly says: ***"through Faith we understand that the whole scheme of time and space was created by the Word of God."*** Out of the two versions, my contextual emphasis is placed on ***"worlds were framed by the Word of God."***

The "worlds" there was not the "world"; which is the planet earth, whose equivalence in Greek is "kosmos".

Fortunately, the one under review here is plural – "worlds". Therefore, we will not mix it up with "world" which is "kosmos" i. e. the physical and visible earth of beautiful things. The "worlds" which is "aion" in Greek refers to the ages, times and seasons.

From the explanation given above, you can now read it the emphasised portion as *"... the times were framed by the Word of God..."* Beloved, God has a plan for our times. Therefore, you do not need to leave the times to chance and magic. You need to understand and discover the times and seasons with God's help. You should use the Word of God to design the kind of future you desire. You are to frame and beautify your future because it is now in your hands, not in God's. As the architect of your future and prophet of your destiny, use the revealed Word of God to frame your times. Use the spoken and written Word of God or prophecies that have gone ahead of you. 1 Timothy 1:18 says, *"According to the prophecies which went before on thee, that thou by them mightiest war a good warfare."*

Action Steps for the Creation of the Future

1. Discover the Word of God that reveals the good plan of God for your beautiful future and you as a person. There cannot be a beautiful future without a beautiful you.

2. Think about the future because you are what you think and your thoughts attract both the visible and the invisible. Mind your thought. Nobody will mind you until you mind yourself. The heart of the matter is the matter of the heart. The issues of life proceed from the heart. Talk less, think more.

Professional public and human capital developers, motivational speakers and preachers around the world do not talk like parrots about their private lives. They are men with few words. That is why their words are full of wisdom and power. Those who know the power of words know that words are spirits and carriers of power in the spirit realm. Be a person of few words. Invest the time of being talkative in being productive, just like a statement made by Richard Templar in his book "The Rule of Work": **"all seeing, all knowing, saying little."** Talkative people do not think. **"In the multitudes of words, there is sin"** says Proverbs 10:19. So, engage your mind in productive thinking instead of engaging in activities that add no value to you. If you ask Bishop Oyedepo time and again what his hobbies are, he will tell you reading and thinking. Leaders are thinkers. See the future in your mind.

3. Do not wait for the future to happen or come to you. Walk into it deliberately, intentionally, strategically and

consciously. Live, feel, act and organise your life around it. Be choosy about the kind of people you associate with and the kind of information you receive, your looks etc. Frame and define your future by dreaming continually. After all, nobody or nothing can stop you from dreaming. You do not pay for it, too. Therefore, dream big because dream comes true.

Surround yourself with positive people. No wonder Charlie "Tremendous" Jones once said, "You will be the same person in five years as you are today except for the people you meet and the books you read." I often tell people that one of the greatest blessings God gave me in my life is my friends and mentors. They are blessings that I appreciate, value and do not take for granted. This is because I am never stranded of receiving wisdom from God through them. As you continually evaluate your life, you need wisdom. Write the names of seven most respected people in your life. By the time you finish writing their names, you are simply looking at your future. That is your circle of influence. I was so excited the last time I wrote mine. Napoleon Hill referred to it as "Mastermind Group".

4. Another way by which the future is created is prayer. Prayer is a means of speaking and sowing words into your future, thereby creating it. No wonder when Paul was

sharing with Corinthian believers in his epistle to them, he said: ***"He that speaks in tongues (pray) edifies himself."*** English Standard Version translates the word "edifies" as "building up". This is similar to building an edifice because "edifies" is derived from "edifice", which is a building. In prayer, we cover distances and time in the future. We travel into the future, put things right there, settle a whole lot of things and enjoy access to times in the Spirit.

4

Planning and Time

"Any enterprise is built by wise planning becomes strong through common sense and profits wonderfully by keeping abreast of the facts"

– Proverbs 24:3-4 (The Living Bible Translation)

"A definite mind of what you set out to achieve, common knowledge of what you want to do and planning give flesh to your decision and backed with focus"

- Drama Group, Daystar Christian Centre

You have a strategic and orderly God who created time for everything and every purpose under heaven. You need to have a plan on how to spend the time judiciously based on a workable plan, having known God's plan for it and how it is in sync with His because a life out of plan is always a life out of place; a totally disjointed bone. Thus, you need to have both long-term plans and short-term plans. You need to have a 10- through 40-year plan because the journey of a thousand miles starts with a step. Short-term plans are a part of the big picture of long-term plans. The former is a sizeable bit that determines whether or not the latter is realisable.

"...the devil we want to bind and rebuke is in the details"

Milestones reached in the short term give confidence for the long term. A plan is not a wish; neither is it a wishful thinking. For its realisation, everything must be factored into it. That is why there is an acronym formulated for a good plan called SMART (Specific, Measurable, Attainable, Realistic and Time-bound). Your plan should also be able to answer the purpose question: the "Why" question, so that it will not just be an emotional plan but a result-oriented plan. You must be able to answer why you want to do or buy that thing. Do not be biased. Have a zero-waste attitude or mindset. Do not waste your time and material resources on what does not add any genuine value to your life.

A plan must also be detailed. I mean very detailed. During planning sessions with people, I love telling them that instead of binding and rebuking the devil while implementing their plans, they should be detailed. This is because the devil you want to bind and rebuke is in the details. You need to discover the devil now. Do not overlook anything. You need to foresee unforeseen circumstances. You have no excuse for failure, mediocrity or poor performance. Instead, you should strive for excellence.

A plan is not a goal. A goal is an idea of what God wants you to do and accomplish or the end picture, while a plan is a detailed road map to the attainment of the goal, that is, the step-by-step detailed phases and activities to the endpoint. My pastor once said, "If you don't plan long-term range, you will be managing crisis and will be under undue pressure and stress, feeling like a failure when growth comes." With this, he quoted the Law of Time Perspective which states that "the more time people spend on planning, the higher they rise and the longer they take into consideration while planning." Little wonder Abraham Lincoln said, "Give me six hours to chop down a tree and I will spend the first four sharpening the ax." You will find how biblical it is in Ecclesiastes 10:10: ***"If the iron be blunt and he do***

not whet the edge, then must he put more strength: but Wisdom is profitable to direct."

One of the benefits of planning is the reduction of some unpleasant surprises and deviations. A good plan boosts your confidence level and makes your success measurable. Any success that is not measurable is not success but frustration. You must as well have a system that evaluates performance to know how well or how good you are doing and to make room for improvement or for redress. You also need to have parameters with which you measure it. In the business world, it is called Key Success Factors (KSF) or Key Performance Indicators (KPIs). Some call it Key Business Indicators (KBIs).

Again, your plan must answer the following questions: What exactly do I want to achieve? Why exactly do I want it? How do I plan to achieve it? Who will I need to consult and inform? When will I be achieving this? (Provide answers for deadline).

See below a sample of action plan table.

WHAT (i.e. What do you want to achieve?)	WHY (Why do you want it?)	HOW (How do you want to go about achieving it?)	WHO (Who will be RACI-responsible, accountable, consulted and informed?) – Mainly, who will be responsible?	When (Due Date/Deadline)

Dear Esteemed Reader, be organised if you do not want to agonise. Do not wait till you are close to the time before you plan for it. Plan now that you are still very far from it.

Gbenga Odunlami

5

"Who Are You?"

Before "How Old Are You?"

Self-discovery is a great pointer to success. A successful person is one who can clearly state their personal creed and values. They must be able to expressly state who they are and who they are not. Therein lies their identity.

I remember the day Pastor Nike Adeyemi was explaining the necessity of defining who we are and who we are not. At a point, she said, "I am a woman, not a man; a wife, not a husband; a mother, not a father; a child of God, not a child of the devil. I'm the righteousness of God, not a sinner." Robert Kiyosaki, in his classic book "Rich Dad, Poor Dad", claims that the most powerful weapon of the

Chinese is the mirror. To them, the mirror represents self-discovery and answers questions about their personality type, passion, interest, ability, source of encouragement and discouragement, purpose, vision, thought, innate quality, gifting, talent and value. Going forward, these define their success.

"...everybody is useful and seedful and must be rightly planted to be fruitful"

With respect to eternity, you should endeavour to identify your gift, potential, installed capacity and inward treasures. God did not create a non-entity. Nobody is useless and irrelevant. Everybody is useful and productive. You need to understand that you have to be rightly planted to be fruitful, that is, turning your seed into fruit requires initial planting. Wrong planting leads to destiny abortion and distortion.

Dear Beloved, you are not a biological accident or a mistake. God knew you before you were formed. He equipped you with all it takes to make it in life. That is why whenever there is a problem, we should look inward before looking outward. Know your worth. I always tell people that success or failure depends on God and me, not the devil. The vision of who you are and the work God has placed in your hands, with which you measure your lifetime, are very crucial to living. Without them, there is nothing to live for. A man living for nothing and without a divine purpose is a dangerous man and a victim of every evil circumstance. My friend, your job is not the same as your purpose, except you have made your purpose your job. Though you may start there, do not stay there. That is not your destination and destiny; neither is it the end for which you were born. Many missionaries are lost and trapped in the career market in different industries today because of material things.

Dear Esteemed Reader, your provision is in your vision. The earlier you believe it, the better it is. Your assignment also determines a lot about you. It determines your choice of friends, places you go, things you do etc. You were created, born and saved for something that had been said concerning you before the foundation of the world. With that assignment comes every necessary tool that you were equipped with right from the beginning. You just need to learn how to use the equipment. I urge you to discover the purpose of your creation.

When God created you, He had something in His mind. He furnished you with everything needed not to be stranded. That is why you are complete in Him. God foresaw a problem you must solve and the need that only you can meet, a vacuum that you must fill in the world, a generation that you must serve according to His will and designed you to do them. Get to work now!

Never think of another replacement or substitute in His purpose and counsel for your life. Discover the vision of God for your life. Every other thing does not matter to God except your vision. Apostle Paul, in his epistle to the Colossian church, said: ***"And say to Archippus, Take heed to the ministry which you have received in the Lord, that you may fulfill it"*** (Colossians 4:17). The Message Translation reads: ***"And oh yes tell Archippus, Do your best in the job you received from the Master. Do your very best"***. Try to fulfil divine destiny because your judgement, appraisal and evaluation depend on it.

If you have been ordained and designed by God to fulfil Task A, but you go ahead to do task B with the whole of your heart, time and resources, it is a waste of time to God. For you not to live a wasted life, you need to discover your assignment. It is very good to discover it early in life because the earlier you get on the right assignment, the earlier your rise. It is never late to turn in the right direction. Again, where there is no vision, people perish. You need to know why you are here on earth. Do not live here purposelessly. Do not be sleeping, waking up, eating, and doing businesses that are not purpose-relevant. Do not live here without any bearing. Stop being involved in everything. Stand for something. Live for something. Live for what you will be known for after you have gone. Live for impact. It is high time you started to live out your installed capacity and maximise your potential. Until you discover and begin to walk in your God-given assignment, you will continue to live in asylum.

"...for you not to live a wasted life, you need to discover your assignment"

Every provision for life is in your vision. Many people live aimlessly in life, without a sense of direction. You need to identify your calling and purpose in life. From God's perspective, they are irrevocable. That is why Paul, in Romans 11:29, said that ***"the gift and the calling of God is without repentance."***

Having material acquisitions is not a yardstick for destiny fulfilment. It is in solving the problems God sent you to the world to solve, helping people God sent you to help and meeting a specific need in the world that you fulfil your purpose. Friend, do not be myopic or short-sighted. Your destiny is more than where you are at the moment. Do not be deceived. Wake up from your slumber and discover your purpose for living. Stop wasting the precious time that God has given to you to fulfil His purpose for your life. Your career is not your destiny, but your destiny can become your career. Stop being busy and guilty. Discover your SHAPE (spiritual gift, heartbeat, ability and personality) and your purpose.

The foregoing acronym is described in Rick Warren's "Purpose-Driven Life" as a 5-pointer to your destiny. It is the SHAPE God gave you at creation and the way God wired or designed you for the fulfilment of your assignment in life. That is why you need to look inward when you are trying to discover your calling in life.

Your **spiritual gifts** could be a pointer to your calling. Apostle Paul, in his letter to the church in Corinth, stated the nine gifts of the Spirit given to every believer as God wills, not as they will. These include gift of prophecy, discerning of spirits, word of wisdom, word of knowledge, gift of interpretation of tongues, gift of diverse kind of tongues, gift of faith, working of miracles and gifts of healings.

Your **heartbeat** is your passion; your strong interest. It is the problem God ordained you to solve. It gives you concern anytime you see it and makes you feel like you have the solution. For example, one of my friends used to say that he detested ignorance and that he always felt like breaking people's heads and filling them up with knowledge. Though it may sound funny, it is nothing short of making a heartbeat statement. Some people hate it when people are unemployable and jobless. They always want to empower them with the right and accurate information needed to secure good jobs and create jobs and wealth. Many issues of concern, interest and passion are too numerous to handle for people bearing some of these specific burdens for their world and generation.

Your **ability** is your can-do, that is, things that flow freely from you without stress or struggle. My advice here is this, if your ability is the surest pointer to your calling in life, work on it and refine it. Do not be crude in your approach to refining it. Make it marketable, valuable and attractive by refining it with skills acquisition and training in that line of potential and ability. Nobody buys or uses crude oil. It is only when it is refined that it becomes acceptable and useful. Do not be a useless man who is full of unrefined potential. Work on yourself. Take courses related to your ability. You will appreciate God and me for acting on this advice.

Your **personality** represents who you are. Who you are is also a pointer to your destiny. Your personality type, whether you are an introvert or extrovert, is one of the courses offered in Level 1 of Leadership Training in our ministry. It is called ***Discovering Your Personality Type and Your Ministry Gift***. The most exciting aspect of the course is the Personality Test administered to soon-to-be developed leaders. A friend once told me that studying such a great course in Level 1 is too early. In response, I told him how helpful it is for us to learn the kind of person we are dealing with right from the beginning. Knowing their abilities after administering the test avails us of the opportunity to place them in different service capacities.

> *"Discovering divine purpose makes your vocation a vacation because you will be involved in what gives you pleasure"*

Lastly, your **experience**, whether good or bad, is a strong pointer to your assignment in life. Specifically, the bad experience you have points to the fact that God is using your mess as a message to prevent other people from going through similar cases and make up leeway for those that are already in it. I have seen people who, after overcoming marital challenges, went on to help those with similar issues, as called by God. Though Peter denied Jesus, he got restored and strengthened others, raising a lot of disciples in the process. I have also heard powerful sermons on how to overcome sexual abuse from victims of rape.

On the other hand, your good experience may be a discoverer of destiny. For instance, having a nice time in business, marriage, academics etc., gives you the confidence to share with people that are having challenges in those areas and aspects of life the productive principles one always works with. Your childhood experience is a strong pointer, too. Since your mind has not been corrupted, it will be easy for you to be playing out the divinely programmed script and capacities meant for you.

I remember when I was 5 years old or thereabouts, I used to organise church services with other children in the neighbourhood. We would pray, sing, dance and I would preach the Word of God while they listened. I would make handmade bills, drawing myself on them and painting them with crayons of different beautiful colours. We would contribute money to cook. As young as we were then, we used to visit the sick and prayed for them. Some people—who saw the seed of greatness in me--kept tabs on my spiritual development and never stopped praying for me since then That is one of the funniest but greatest experiences that the Holy Spirit called my attention to while He was speaking to me about ministry some years ago,

Since God is the Owner of your life, you need to ask Him exactly what He wants you to do with your life, regardless of all the obvious pointers. Discovering divine purpose makes your vocation a vacation, as you will be involved in what gives you pleasure. What problems are you ordained to solve? What needs are you ordained to meet? What questions are you ordained to answer? To God, success in life is destiny-defined and destiny-measured. It is not measured by the amount of money you have in your bank account or the number of houses you have built. Do not misinterpret my stance on this. It is not a cover up or an excuse for poverty, since our financial prosperity enhances the fulfilment of our assignment. The truth about our life's success is that it is measured by how we are fulfilling our God-given destinies and assignments in life.

Section 2

Principle-Centred Living

Running Lawfully

"[24]Do you not know that those who run in a race all run, but one receives the prize? Run in such a way that you may obtain it, [25]and every one who competes for the prize is temperate in all things, now they do it to obtain a perishable crown, but we for an imperishable crown, [26]therefore I run thus: not with uncertainty, thus I fight not as one who beats the air"

(1 Corinthians 9:24-26, NKJV).

"And also if anyone competes in athletics, he is not crowned unless he competes according to the rules"

(2 Timothy 2:5, NKJV).

Principles are unarguably timeless, unchangeable and irreversible truths which have been proven and tested over time. They are universally acceptable and functional.

Never live your life as one that beats the wind, but according to rules. There are principles, rules and laws that guide success. If you live based on them, you will surely come out successful. I will share some of them which I have applied in my little walk in life in the next chapter.

6

The Rule of Knowledge

"For the Lord is the God of knowledge and by Him actions are weighed"

- 1 Samuel 2:3

I define knowledge as a knowing that gives you an edge, that is, the result of splitting the word knowledge into two: **KNOW** and **EDGE**.

Knowledge acquisition could come formally or informally. Secularly called "education," it has its etymology in the Latin word "educo," which means "educing from within." John C. Maxwell said, "Education is not adding to a pail but igniting a fire." This description means a lot, one of which portrays education as one that brings to limelight the potential within. It should be a process of refining and converting raw gifts to a well-packaged and marketable skill. This suggests that our educational system should be real and practical.

In fact, whoever has not discovered themselves should not be exposed to education given the fact that many of us have done some courses that have no intentional, deliberate and conscious relevance to our purpose, assignment and destiny. Had we expended all our resources and time on our relevant place of assignment, we would have been better off and well positioned for greatness in our prime.

> *"I define knowledge as a knowing that gives you an edge"*

Knowledge gives you an edge not only above your peers, competitors or colleagues at workplace but also above challenges of life and issues in your marriage, finance, career, ministry etc. I discovered that Hosea 4:6 is not read as ***"My people are destroyed for lack of prayer but lack of knowledge."*** No wonder Bishop Oyedepo once said, "There are no mountains anywhere; every man's ignorance is his mountain." Therefore, we should not be ignorant. Grace and peace become multiplied through knowledge (2 Peter 1:2), while the just always get delivered through knowledge (Proverbs 11:9). Even in John 8:32, Jesus made us understand that freedom hinges on the truth that you know. ***"You shall know the truth and the truth shall make you free,"*** He said. Therefore, knowledge is critical to success in life.

Someone defined "LUCK" as Labouring under Correct Knowledge. So, it is not just being fortunate or lucky. It is knowledge that makes you to be preferred and acceptable. This hugely depends on the power of information, the force that drives a vision. It takes relevant information to fully deliver the details of any vision. If you do not have respect for knowledge, you may not go far in life. Every committed fact hunter ends up being a pacesetter.

"...every great vision demands a great knowledge investment"

"The devil is as powerful to the level of your ignorance," my pastor once declared, adding that if one is too old to learn, one is really too old. Ignorance is a powerful aging factor in this part of the world. People are not learning; neither are they taking up new challenges. They are not embracing new opportunities. You cannot be too old to learn. When you stop learning, you stop living. When you stop living, you start dying.

Brian Sher in his book "What Rich People Know and Desperately Want to Keep Secret" said, "Education is the shortcut to success." While he was explaining this salient point, he challenged business people who do not go for seminars, conferences and courses and revealed the two major reasons for their unwillingness to acquire knowledge from the foregoing places: pride and comfort. Stop being too comfortable and complacent. Never be at ease with your accomplishment. It should either be that you are always pursuing something or something is pursuing you. You cannot afford to be at ease for nothing, even if you are waiting patiently for a miracle or breakthrough. Waiting is not an excuse for time wasting.

Early on, I intimated that waiting time should not be a wasting time. Instead, it should be a loading time, a time of preparing for a great opportunity that lies ahead. Bishop Oyedepo, in his response to a man who told him to take it easy at the inception of his now globally known ministry (Living Faith Church), popularly known as Winners' Chapel, said, "Those who took it easy yesterday have been eased out."

Pride is the second of the two reasons Brian Sher gave as a threat to personal development. Dear Esteemed Reader, always be humble, simple, and meek in order to learn. Only ***"the meek He will show His way"*** **(Psalm 25:9)** and ***"The entrance of His Word will***

always give light and understanding only to the simple (Psalm 119:130)." Be meek and teachable.

Many people who ought to learn and listen today for a trans-generational leadership command have lost their way because they always want to talk. They end up preaching to their instructor because they think that they know it all. In their arrogance, they do not bother to take notes while learning. For instance, when an arrogant person sees a handbill or invitation to attend a seminar or study a course, they foolishly criticise it with analysis, saying: "Oh, this subject of faith! I know everything about it" or "Oh, that computer application! I know everything about it."

Do not compete with the person you should learn from; rather, you should honour them. In fact, my own definition of ignorance is not only lack of knowledge but also an act of ignoring and despising knowledge. It stems from "ignore", its derivative.

Once, I had an experience made me to understand the concept of ignorance. I went to an IT training centre to make enquiries about some of their advanced courses because I felt that I needed to take one. On the list I was given, I saw a programme/course on a business application in use where one of my friends was working.

This was an application they used for business transactions. When I discovered that its cost was on the high side, I heaved a deep sigh and told the lady attendant that until one loses what one has, one will not know the value, adding that one does not know the value of what one has until one is informed about its worth. I said this, knowing fully well that that was an application some staff members of an organisation would grumble to learn when asked to be trained. What a true picture of ignorance!

Pastor Chris Oyakhilome of the Believers' Loveworld, popularly known as Christ Embassy, once gave a perfect illustration of value. Implicitly, he explained how knowledge helps one to appreciate the value of what one has. He said that one may have been using a pen gifted to one by someone for a long time without appreciating its worth. By chance, one meets a man who informs one about how expensive that pen is and how it is not easily accessible to the extent that only three people have it in the world. This includes one and two other persons. It is this new information that will change the status of the pen from what it used to be: one will definitely appreciate the worth of the pen thenceforward.

One of my favourite sayings any time I talk about vision and the necessity of knowledge for the fulfilment of vision goes thus: "Every great vision demands a great knowledge investment." Training, which includes human capital development, investment in knowledge and retraining, is one of the secrets of great organisations, companies and businesses around the world. They spend so much on training. Organisations, for instance, conduct induction or training on the first day at work for new employees because they cannot afford to risk their deficient information or misinformation about the company's vision, culture, values, policies and position on some critical business issues. Why this is done is that knowledge saves one from stress, downtime, loss time and loss of money. No wonder they say knowledge is power.

While reading some books about Toyota's culture and values some years ago, I could see how the organisation places premium on training and development of her employees. Little wonder a wise man once said, "Training turns a trash to a treasure, and training leads to reigning." No organisation or church ministry can grow beyond her staff members and what they know. Poor performance is as a result of poor knowledge communication. Individuals cannot do what they do not know. As a leader, do not assume that they should know when you have not empowered them. Knowledge positions people for discernment and accurate judgement. It stabilises individuals. This is because, as I discovered, lack of knowledge leads to making unstable decisions.

A reader today is not only a leader but also a writer tomorrow. With inspiration, they write from the abundance of what they have read, having been consistently exposed to thoughts in great books for years.

Dear Esteemed Reader, you have to read your way up. Knowledge transforms. It changes you from inside out. That is why information is in-formation, forming you from within. Knowledge not only prevents you from problems but also solves them. Solutions to a million naira problem may be in a ten thousand naira book or seminar.

I often tell my mentees that books are tools in the school of practical greatness. People cannot perform more than their knowledge capacity. Remember, Paul was an ardent reader. While he was writing to Timothy, he said, "Bring my books." Daniel was also a bookworm. Scripture makes us understand that "Daniel understood by books." Even Jesus read a lot.

Beloved, the solution to a long-term problem in your life may be in a book you are seeing everyday but ignoring.

Do not forget my definition of ignorance: "ignoring knowledge." The Book of Proverbs 23:9 says, ***"The fear of the Lord is the beginning of knowledge, but fools despise wisdom and discipline."*** Do not be a fool. One thing that I have observed is when we are praying to God to give us what has already been given or lies around us unpossessed and untapped as opportunities waiting to be grasped, He uses knowledge to make us see that He has answered our prayers. Learn to improve your knowledge daily. Learning determines your earning. Empty your purse on your head. Alvin Tofler said, "The illiterates of the 21st century are not those who cannot read nor write, but those who cannot learn, unlearn and relearn those things that they have learnt before."

Be ready to learn. Learning is continuous. It is a daily job, not a day's job. The person you are learning from may make jest of you. Just endure it. Absorb it for the moment. Nothing is permanent. With time, you will gain mastery over the subject.

A learner today is a leader tomorrow. An apprentice today is a trainer or an instructor tomorrow. Knowledge makes the difference. It is not too late to go back to school to take a relevant course. You can learn from anybody, listen to corrections and instructions from people and get inspired by the written Word of God. The Bible, according to 2 Timothy 3:16-17, is for correction and rebuke, not only to excite us. I wonder what would have happened to Captain Naman if he had disregarded the advice of his servant to do what Elisha asked him to do. Maybe he would have been a great captain with a "but" (leprosy) for life (2 Kings 5:1-14).This happens to a lot of people today. They do not listen to God speaking to them through their spouses, friends, subordinates, children and associate pastors. They are headstrong. Proverbs 29:1 says, ***"He who is often rebuked, and hardens his neck will suddenly be destroyed, and that without remedy."***

Another benefit of knowledge is that it helps you to understand people, places, things and issues better. I remember when I read the book "The Mafia Manager," I saw the reasons behind many senior managers' actions and words. Sincerely, reading the following books: Understanding the Power and Purpose of Woman; His Needs, Her Needs; and Men Are from Mars, Women Are from Venus made me understand some things about women generally. They knocked out some funny ideologies I had ignorantly learnt about women.

Soft Skills and Competence

One of the remarkable things I saw in Jacob's response to Pharaoh's question "How old are you?", in Genesis 47:9, is this statement: ***"Few and evil have been the days of the years of my life."*** The New International Version of the statement reads: ***"My years have been few and difficult"***, while The Message translation says, ***"A short and hard life"***.

Ignorance always makes things difficult. If you want to know how knowledge softens a hard life or dissolves difficulty, the different versions of Ecclesiastes come in handy.

"Who is like the wise? Who knows the explanation of things? A person's wisdom brightens their face and changes its hard appearance" (New International Version);

"How wonderful to be wise, to analyze and interpret things. Wisdom lights up a person's face, softening its harshness'" (New Living Translation).

"Who is like the wise? And who knows the interpretation of a thing? A man's wisdom

makes his face shine, and the hardness of his face is changed" (English Standard Version).

"Who is like the wise man? Who knows the interpretation of a matter? A man's wisdom brightens his face, and the sternness of his face is changed" (Berean Study Bible).

"Who is like the wise man and who knows the interpretation of a matter? A man's wisdom illumines him and causes his stern face to beam" (New American Standard Bible).

"Who is like a wise man? And who knows the interpretation of a thing? A man's wisdom makes his face shine. And the sternness of his face is changed" (New King James Version).

"Who is like the wise person, and who knows the interpretation of a matter? A person's wisdom brightens his face, and the sternness of his face is changed" (Christian Standard Bible).

"Who is smart enough to explain everything? Wisdom makes you cheerful and gives you a smile" (Contemporary English Version)

"Only the wise know what things really mean. Wisdom makes them smile and makes their frowns disappear" (Good News Translation).

"Who is like the wise person, and who knows the interpretation of a matter? A man's wisdom brightens his face, and the sternness of his face is changed" (Holman Christian Standard Bible).

"Who is really wise? Who knows how to interpret this saying: "A person's wisdom improves his appearance, softening a harsh countenance?" (International Standard Version)

"Who is a wise person? Who knows the solution to a problem? A person's wisdom brightens his appearance, and softens his harsh countenance" (NET Bible).

"Who is like the wise man? And who knows the interpretation of a thing? A man's wisdom makes his face shine, and the hardness of his face is changed" (New Heart English Bible).

One of the benefits of revival and advancement of knowledge in this age is "ease." Another word I can use for it is the opposite word for "hard" which is "soft." No wonder we have soft touch, software etc. The cure to hard work is soft skills acquisition. I personally know what it is to do a hard work. I mean hard work and menial work. I will encourage you to acquire a soft skill and go for global knowledge.

If you ignore mental development, you are automatically signing up for a menial employment. Therefore, develop skills, expertise and competence in your discipline. Know more about the subject. He who is diligent and competent will be qualified for the palace job. From the word of King Pharaoh in the latter part of our central scriptural passage which reads: ***"If you know any competent men among them, make them chief herdsmen over my livestock"(Genesis 47:6),*** you get to see the group, among the covenant people of God, that can be in charge of the royalty investment and business. Ignorance is appalling, Apostle Paul, while replying to the Corinthian church letter in 1st Corinthians 12 verse 1, says: ***"Concerning spiritual gifts, I will not have you to be ignorant"***. The word "ignorant" there could be defined as lack of information, wrong information or misinformation.

Assumption is also one of the costliest, most foolish and stupidest ways of learning. You assume when you do not know something or do not know enough of something and you claim that you know it. Paul also said in 2

Corinthians 2:11 that believers should not take chances or risk being ignorant of the devices of the devil, their archenemy.

Books! Books! Books!

One of the reasons why I am passionate about this is because it is one of my top personal core values and number one core value in our ministry. I detest ignorance. Proverbs 19:2 says, ***"For a soul to be without knowledge, it is not good."***

As a voracious reader, I use every opportunity I have to read. You cannot see me without a book. I buy books with the conviction that there will be a need for its manifestation in my life someday. The mind is such a powerful tool that replays everything you know about every pressing issue. Therefore do not say you do not need it now. Just keep reading it.

I pity people who spend thousands or millions of naira to prepare for wedding ceremonies without having a single book on marriage, family building and parenting. Many who complain about their health but do not have a single book on health management have tens or hundreds of books on financial management, business management, success strategies etc.

I had an experience while I was preparing to get married. As I was praying one morning, the Holy Spirit told me to get all the books on marriage and family building, ever written by Mama Faith Oyedepo of the Living Faith Church Worldwide and read them. I jumped out of my house to get those volumes immediately at the Canaan Land Bookshop. I must say that getting and reading those books as well as other books prepared me and my spouse for marriage.

Shortly after then, I bought books that enhance the role of a minister's wife as gifts for my wife. Books such as Mama Faith Oyedepo's "The Effective Minister's Wife" and Oretha Hagin's "The Price is not Greater than the Grace". Both books have been blessings to my family since I bought them. They have tremendously helped us.

I remember that I started reading books on parenting when I was in the university. That is why I said early on that you should never say that you do not need it or you cannot afford to buy it. If it requires sacrifice to get it, you have to. Then, I would spend all my money on books and tapes. Same thing happened when I started working and was still single. I bought more books than foodstuff. At some point, buying clothes was out of my plan. I believed so much in eating (reading) those books. Sincerely, that was the degree of my passion for knowledge acquisition. I am saying all this to revive your passion for knowledge.

Many years ago, I heard a man who said that if his library was sold, the money would buy five powerful new model Jeep cars. Once, a great man of God in Nigeria, who was moving into a new house, engaged the service of Packers Company. After offering their service, the company had to confess that they had never done what they did in his former house since the inception of the company: spending three days to pack books in his library after packing his baggage, gadgets, furniture etc. effortlessly. That was the extent to which he went in acquiring knowledge. Little wonder his greatness is enviable.

Learning from the Successful

If you see anybody thriving more than you do in your line of business or ministry, a colleague excelling at workplace, doing well with a skill of your own interest, an individual having a healthy financial life, a good family and parenting, the truth is, there is something that person knows and does that you don't. That is the edge they have over you. This best explains my definition of knowledge. Do not criticise them. The knowledge they have is the extra that adds up to their ordinariness and makes them extraordinary. Move closer to the person. Hear them speak. While they speak, listen to them with rapt attention to learn from them the secret behind their extraordinariness. Bury your pride. Attend their seminars. Ask them questions when you have the opportunity. Read their books, if they have written any. Make sure you get something about the person. Listen to their recorded messages on CDs or tapes and listen to them repeatedly. Buy the truth from them. Do not be stingy to your destiny. Book an appointment with them, if given the opportunity, but do not waste their time. Doing this will earn you more respect from them, especially when you show respect to their time. This is because they have other things to attend to. Write questions you want to ask before meeting them. Trying to remember subject of discussion right in their presence is insulting.

Different Learning Styles

Before I conclude this great chapter, let me share something I read about learning modalities in Anthony Parinello's "Think and Sell Like a CEO" with you to bail you out of frustrations. As we have different personality styles, so have we learning styles or learning modalities. Some people learn best by pictures, while some learn best by hearing and listening. Not all of us will be book reading experts. That is why we have audio books, audio Bibles etc.

Anthony Parinello, in this book, stated that there are three primary learning styles: visual (seeing is believing), auditory (I can hear what you are saying) and kinaesthetic (I've got a good feeling about this). Visual learners prefer visual simulations and visual displays; auditory learners want to listen to the words being said and the way the entire message is being delivered. They are very sensitive to the pitch, tone and volume of the communicator's voice, while kinaesthetic learners put a premium on emotional connection- feelings and person-to-person contact.

7

The Rule of Action Orientation

"Fear looks, faith jumps"

- Smith Wigglesworth

Dear Esteemed Reader, many people called executives today are not executing anything. They are just collecting fat salaries. Without working on your plans, they are as good as dead. You need to take steps. Until you take the first step, you may not know how possible it is for you to take the next one. The world serves those who have made up their mind and are fully committed to a cause. Nothing moves until you move it. Procrastination is the enemy of action orientation. It belongs to the same group with laziness and complacency. Nothing in life is stationary. Life itself is not. It moves every second, bringing along change. That is why you have to be proactive. See thousands of miles from where you stand and keep moving.

"...your plans without working on them is as good as dead" I always tell my church members that their goals for the New Year will not jump out of paper and fulfil themselves. They are the ones that must leave their comfort zones, stop daydreaming and wishful thinking and make things work. Nothing works until you work it out. Even Jesus, while on earth, was a worker. In John 5:17, He said, ***"My Father works hitherto and I work."*** The Almighty God Himself also worked out the planned creation that was on his mind for six days and rested on the seventh day. Work must precede rest. Things will not fall on your laps forever. The price for excellence is diligence. Go out and pay it. You have sat on that chair for long, planning and speculating. It is time to rise up and work it out. Arise and shine! No wonder Ecclesiastes 10:15 says, ***"The labour of the foolish man wearies him for he does not know how to go to the field."*** You have waited for too long. Take that bold step of faith. Act with boldness.

It is the doer that is blessed. Never be satisfied with your present status. Never be complacent. A wise man said, "Progress is never the work of contented people." The same man defined quality as a result of high intention, sincere effort, intelligent direction and skilful execution.

During the break session at a leadership conference, I was looking at my pastor from a distance as he was chatting and laughing with his wife while they were seeing off some family friends out of their office unit. I thought to myself: "These people are human beings like me. They are Nigerians like me, of the same tribe. They are ordinary men like me but are doing great things and have been on it consistently for a long period of time, taking steps courageously. They stepped out in faith out of their comfort zones." We just have to ACT and use every window of opportunity.

Focus is also important in action orientation. Until you are focused, you are not a focus. Focus on the result while undergoing the process. One of the clear definitions of focus is deliberate and selective neglect. Be focused. You cannot be driving a car forward while looking backward, except you have decided to be a victim of a fatal accident. There are always some agitation, tension and pains when you are about to give birth to something great. Endure the pain. Delay gratifications. Be forward looking. I am glad I did is better than I wish I'd done.

Make hay while the sun shines and take that leap now. Start from where you are with what you have. Do not despise the days of small beginnings. A Chinese proverb says, "Even great towers start at ground level." This is corroborated by the words of B. C. Forbes which says, "If you don't drive your business, you will be driven out of business."

"*...the price for excellence is diligence*" Nothing moves until you move it. Nothing changes until you change it. Nothing works until you work it out. The extra you do which others don't do makes you extraordinary. Go the extra mile. Stretch yourself. I like what Bill Rancic, the winner of Donald Trump's first edition of The Apprentice, said in his book "You're Hired": "There are no secret to success but working harder than the guy next to you, thinking smarter than the guy next to you, and wanting it just a little more than the guy next to you."

Obedience to God and faith also exemplify action orientation. Conversely, disobedience and fears are enemies of action orientation. Discouragement here and there is also one of the things that hinder people from taking action. Here is my advice: you should not be discouraged. Never give up or give in. As long as you are on a journey to fulfil what God said about you, you can count on Him and His Word. Do not be discouraged at all. Apostle Paul, in 2 Corinthians 4:1, said, ***"Therefore, since we have this ministry, as we have received mercy we do not lose heart."*** The Living Bible Translation of Proverbs 24:10 reads: ***"You are a poor specimen if you can't stand the pressure of adversity."***

> ***"Today must be better than yesterday anyway anyhow"***

Keep moving. You may not know how close you are to success until you turn back. So, do not be discouraged. Keep making progress. That is your destiny. Dean Karnazes said, "Run when you can, walk if you have to, crawl if you must; just never give up." Keep getting better. It may be a 1% improvement. Just keep improving and advancing. It is dangerous to be stagnant or stationary. Today should be better than yesterday.

Caution Note: As good as it is to move and act, patience has to be considered. I like the last part of Isaiah 28:16 which reads: ***"Whoever believes will not act hastily."*** Have a staying power. Be calm. Persevere.

8

The Rule of Environment

Your environment has a way of influencing your way of life and reasoning. No matter how good your seed is, the quality of the soil environment determines whether or not it will grow. Sometimes, when God wants to change a man, He will reposition him from his present environment to a better one to upgrade his thought pattern and model to fit into His plan for him. Many people are out of an environment, but the environment has yet to be out of them. The oppressive Pharaoh understood this principle. That is why he insisted on allowing the children of Israel to worship their God, but would not allow them to go far away from Egypt. He knew that if they left Egypt, they would be free from oppression.

When you stay in an environment for a period of time, its composition will affect your culture, language or choice of word and value systems, except you choose not to allow it to influence you. The kind of environment you expose your mind to, where you live and where you visit affect your vision and envisioning capacity. Take action to visit environments more beautiful, prosperous and organised than yours. You will see that you will aspire higher and think better. The kind of school environment your children learn from at their tender age goes a long way in affecting them as they grow up. That sums up their background. Excellence-oriented schools will enlarge their intellectual capacity. They will grow up with prosperity and abundance mindset, not scarcity mindset. They will think and dream big. In such an environment, they will rub shoulders with peers with royalty mindset.

"You may be in a third world environment but live in the first world environment with your mindset"

Dear Esteemed Reader, if you want to change your life, change your environment. Another way of seeing this subject of environment is to import a better environment, that is, go for excursions at your leisure time. It is pathetic that, in this part of the world, many of our leaders travel to developed nations but cannot replicate what they see there in their underdeveloped and developing nations. I am not sure whether their eyes of understanding are open anytime they travel to those great places.

Though you may not change your geographical location, you can make where you are as beautiful as those places you have visited and whose images you have captured though observation and picture-taking. After all, there is learning by observation and image is critical to success.

Visuals and pictures affect our imaginations. What we see consistently over a period of time --the clean, beautiful and well-organised environment--affects our imagination. Imagination is defined as image formation because what you see is what you get and become. You may be in a Third World environment but live in the First World environment with your mindset. It is your choice to change your environment to what you want.

Though Joseph was in prison, his mindset was never imprisoned. He chose not to allow the prison to be in him. He lived the palace in the prison, solving problems with his gift, a sign of his eventual crowning as prime minister. Though Paul and Silas were chained, they were praising God as if they had been freed. In the twinkling of an eye, God repositioned them to the environment they internally created for themselves. Paul lived the most impactful moment of his life writing many of his epistles while in prison. He never allowed the restriction that the prison offered to weigh him down. He wasted no time. He maximised the season and his solitude, writing and preaching to destinies tied to his loins by God.

9

The Rule of Association

"Be not deceived: evil communication corrupt good manners"
(1 Corinthians 15:33).

"He who walks with the wise will be wise, but the companion of fools will be destroyed"
(Proverbs13:20).

"You will be the same person in five years as you are today except for the people you meet and the books you read"
- Charlie "Tremendous" Jones.

Your association determines a whole lot about you. Someone once said, "Your friends determine your end." Conversely, I say, "Your end determines your friends." Friendship is not by force but by choice. It is where you are going in life that determines who you pick as friends, the kind of things you buy and do. A mature person keeps relationships while an immature persons breaks theirs. Someone said that you may not know the king, but you need to know someone who knows the person who knows the king.

Relationship is key. Association comprises your upward, horizontal and downward relationships. Upward relationship constitutes those whom you look up to (mentors, fathers and instructors); horizontal relationship constitutes your peers, friends and colleagues; and downward relationship constitutes people who look up to you (protégés, sons, daughters, apprentices, associates and destinies attached to your loins by divine arrangement).

Association determines the fulfilment of your destiny. That is why I always tell people that they cannot fulfil destiny in isolation. Even Jesus, while on earth, was not found lonely. He was always with God (His Father) whenever He went up the mountain to pray. God loves interaction. He enjoys being with us. Thus, He calls us into fellowship with Himself.

Boredom and isolation kill destinies. You need associations. God speaks to you many times through your network. The Bible account of the early apostles reveals that when they were released from chains, they went to their own company (Acts Chapter 4:23-24). This shows how much they cherish their company (people that they can confide in; people that can encourage them in faith; and people who will make them see their predicament with positive lens). In Daniel 2:16:17, Daniel went to his own company when he was confronted with a difficult puzzle. Your company can make or break you. You have the choice to either influence or be influenced. You should also be honest and plain to your companions. The concluding part of Acts 4:23 says, ***"...and they reported all."*** Your companions should be people who are not bitter, intimidated and insecure about your progress. They should be people who are ready to share your problems with you and proffer solutions to them, not pretenders who feel sorry in your presence but express how happy they are that you have problems after you have left or technical witches or wizards saddened by your success.

Beware of mentors and friends who think and act like this, too. Over the years, they have successfully made victims out of their mentees and friends. When these folks eventually wriggle free from the grips of their oppressors, they claim God and the Holy Spirit are their mentors and friends. I advise you to be selective and prayerful when choosing your mentor and friend. Allow God to lead you through the selection process. You did not choose your biological parents; neither should you for your spiritual parents. God determined it. Leave this to God. Let Him lead you by Himself. The mentor you want to be like or someone you want to befriend may not look or act like a traitor.

Up until now, I have a mentor whose attention was initially hard to get. I tried all I could and almost gave up. *"...every star has a coach"* Then, God always assured me that my destiny was attached to his loins any time I prayed. Once, I told God that I was not sure he was available for me and that his life was not connected with mine. In His response, He told me to keep following him.

Dear Esteemed Reader, your company is very critical to your success in life. I advise you to get mentors and friends that will accelerate your journey. Forget about prejudice or age difference. Learn from your mentors. Appreciate them. Give them gifts. Serve them. Be open to them. Be intimate with them. Speak positively about them. Be loyal to them. Never equate yourself with them. Identify with them proudly. People who do not have mentors are preys to tormentors. Those who do not have fathers are destiny orphans. They do not go far in life. Mentors accelerate the journey to your destination. Even if you see any weakness or flaw in them, call their attention to it politely. Understand the fact that there are no perfect human beings; and that we are all working towards perfections. After all, you also have your own area of weakness. Therefore, respect your mentor as your father. Tell them the truth but in the spirit of love. Your father will always be your father. Do not be an arrogant, unattached gloomy star. Every star has a coach, be it a sports star, academic star etc. Your star cannot manifest until you are accountable to an instructor, a coach, mentor, guide and father.

Your mentor depicts or reflects your future. Their achievements show you the possibility of the vision given to you by God. If you want to be inspired, do not follow those who have expired. Follow those whose lives inspire you. Having a mentor does not give you the liberty to be requesting money or material things from them, though you can collect if they give.

While preparing for my wedding, I needed some amount of money to settle some emergency bills and was advised to tell a mentor to lend me since I had the capacity to refund. I vehemently refused it because my mentor-mentee relationship with him was not meant for receiving money from him but for receiving wisdom and insight. It was not that he could not afford to lend me the money if I did request it. I believed in the insight and wisdom capital that made him who he was and was transacting with him in that line. I never wanted to sever our relationship. I also believed that having the wisdom capital that he had would make me replicate his result repeatedly and would not make me depend on his hand-outs. Again, unhealthy money attachment to relationships sometimes destroys relationships. I have observed that people respect you when you seldom ask or do not ask them for money at all. They go the extra mile to get you juicy opportunities. This shows they are impressed by your position about money.

To mentors out there, you should not be after material and monetary gains from your mentees. I am not saying that you should not receive them when given. That should not be the primary purpose, expectation and intention for the mentor-mentee relationship.

A man of God shared how, for the first time, he sowed a seed to his mentor and got a refund with blessing from the mentor. I love the prophetic theme picture painted by Elisha's statement about Elijah: ***"My father, my father, the chariot of Israel and the horsemen thereof."*** Reading one Bible rendition of this statement, I saw: ***"My father, my father, you are the chariot***

of Israel." Another translation further stresses, saying: ***"My father, my father, you are the Mighty Defender of Israel."***

Learning from a mentor makes you stand on their shoulders to see afar. It helps you not to reinvent the wheel or repeat the mistakes they made in their journey to stardom. You do not have to repeat that mistake. You need to learn from their experience. Build from where they are. Make the journey easier for yourself. Do not make it difficult by ignoring mentoring.

As a mentor, reproduce yourself in your mentee. You groom and build them up for the fulfilment of destiny. Open up your library system to them. Do not hoard information from them. Send them on trainings and seminars. Never be insecure with their surpassing success. Let them redefine your own success. Their success tells the world that you are successful. Every child should be greater than their parents. The greatest investment you can make is investment in human beings.

If you run a system, a church or business organisation, never hesitate to release your protégé, associate and staff member when they ask for it. Do not kill their dreams and visions. Do not delay their destiny. "To him that gives, more will be given to him" and "the liberal soul will be made fat" are the words from Scriptures.

At the inception of our ministry, one of the things that God told me as the set man was that most of the people that He would be sending to me to work with me were for grooming; and that I should never be reluctant to release them whenever they asked to be released. As young as I am in the ministry, I have released some associates. One of them was so dear to me that I became emotional when he announced his departure. He went to plant and pastor a church in a city that was about 6 hours' journey from where I was. In all fairness, I did not brood over the departure of the loyal and reliable son because of what God told me when I started out in ministry.

After releasing and praying for him that fateful afternoon, the Holy Spirit redefined my ministry. God told me that He was happy with my obedience and assured me that He would take my ministry higher. That same day, I got a hold of what the next phase of my ministry would be after having been intimated by the Holy Spirit. It was indeed a great time of meditation for me. Subsequently, I observed that any time my mentee came around for a special meeting in our ministry, he used to say that a lot of things had changed since he left. For me, that was the initial agitation I had when he was leaving as well as fear of the unknown as to what would happen should the faithful associate leave. I learnt a great deal from that experience. Regrettably, many mentors find it challenging to release their trained protégé because of their greed, selfishness and insecurity.

10

The Rule of Image

"But the Lord said to Samuel, Do not look at his appearance or at his physical stature, because I have refused him, for the Lord does not see as man sees; for MAN LOOKS AT THE OUTWARD APPEARANCE, but the Lord looks at the heart"

(1 Samuel 16:7).

There is no point having good content when you have a bad packaging. It is the latter people see before they see the former. Excellence does not agree with doing something anyhow. It is a mindset and an attitude. It does not have to be expensive. It is a function of creativity, thoughtfulness and simplicity. Whatever you invest in excellence will surely come back to you in multiple folds. It is an investment, not an expense. Excellence is also diligence and paying attention to detail.

Lee Kuan Yew, former Singaporean president and the author of the book "From the Third World to the First World," which I read some years ago, shared how he evaluates people's diligence and attention to the minutest detail by looking at the neatness of their footwear. He said if it shines, it shows the person is not carefree or a freelance.

"Excellence does not agree with doing it anyhow"

Always look good. Look after your image: your hair cut, hairdo, nails, clothes, carriage, complimentary card, colour combo, logos, designs, fluency, accent, good command of language, grammatical correctness etc. Do not overlook these things. Christianity is not an excuse for mediocrity. God is an excellent, good-looking, gorgeous and beautiful personality. Anointing is not a cover up for shabby looks. David was a young, anointed and spirit-filled man in the Bible. He had content and his outward appearance was enviable. One of the servants of King Saul described his profile for a job opening in the palace. In his words, found in 1 Samuel 16:18, David" *is skilful in playing, a mighty man of valour, a man of war, prudent in speech and A HANDSOME PERSON and the Lord*

was with him." Moffatt Translation renders the emphasised phrase as ***"a man of good presence,"*** while the Bible in Basic English reads: ***"wise in his words and PLEASING IN HIS LOOKS*.**"

The way you dress is the way you'll be addressed. Your image is determined by your self-image. Your self-Image is determined by your self-esteem. Your self-esteem is determined by your thought. Your thought is determined by your knowledge level, that is, the product of what you see, hear and your environment.

"Christianity is not an excuse for mediocrity"

It is all about how you see yourself based on what you see in yourself and about yourself. If you see the little business you are running as a multinational, you will project the image like that to everyone who comes in contact with it. That is what it will be because image is magnetic.

First impression lasts longer. You may not have the audience or opportunity for a second one. Why not get it right the first time?

11

The Rule of Love

You cannot drive a great destiny without love. It is foundational to success. Without it, you may be pursuing a short-term success. If you want to build a lasting success, love is a non-negotiable requirement. It is at the base of every great business system. One of the slogans of an organisation is founded on care. This is very true because a great business emerges from a man's compassion for the dying world around him. In his quest to save lives, he gets his business redefined and firm to date after tens of decades in many nations of the world, rising while others are crumbling because it is rooted in love. No wonder Theodore Roosevelt made the statement: "Nobody cares how much you know until they know how much you care."

Maturity is action in consideration. Even Jesus' healing ministry had its roots in compassion. A friend defined compassion as "a compound or complex passion." It is the deepest, strongest and highest level of being moved with concern and gravitating towards a need. Compassion acts, while passion feels concerned. Do not just feel sorry about people's problem. Think of what to do to solve it and how to solve the problem. Solve it!

> *"... if you want to build a lasting success, love is a non negotiable requirement"*

We should not love in words only but in actions. Faith without work is dead. A simple modern day-to-day English translation of the Bible statement says, "Faith without corresponding action is dead."

I tell people that business should not first be profit-oriented but solution-oriented. Money accompanies people. Anywhere you see people, you see money. This is because people invented money, not God. As a means of exchanging values, the only thing God gives is idea, productive idea that solves problems and consequently attracts its monetary equivalence. Meet a need. Solve a problem. Answer a question bothering people's heart. Make things easier, faster, cheaper and more comfortable for people. If you are selling tomatoes and the need of the people living where you are is not tomatoes but fish, you are just wasting your time and resources. You are simply not doing any business. It does not matter if that is the kind of business you love to do. As long as it is not meeting anybody's needs, it is a bad business.

People do not mind emptying their purses into your purse if you can meet their dire, pressing and unavoidable needs. Every human being is the extension of God. When the apostles were praying to God to stretch out His arms in the Book of Acts of the Apostles, how did God answer the prayer? He simply used them to do what they asked Him to do, manifesting how they were His outstretched arms in the process. So, treat every human being specially. Everyone is the image of God. Do not do what you cannot do to God to a fellow human being. I love 1 John 4:20 for its vivid explanation of the subject of love: ***"If someone says I love God and he hates his brother, he is a liar, for he who does not love his brother whom he has seen, how can he love God whom he has not seen?"***

Jesus, speaking in Matthew 25: 34 -40, gave an account of what will happen to the righteous of God when He returns in glory. He said, ***"When I was hungry you gave me food. When I was thirsty, you gave me drink. When I was a stranger, you took me in. When I was naked, you clothed me. When I was***

sick, you visited me. When I was in prison, you came to me. Then the righteous will answer Him, saying, 'Lord, when did we see you hungry and feed you or thirsty and give you drink...? ...and the King will say in as much as you did it to one of the least of these my brethren, you did it to me."

No wonder Apostle Paul admonished us to "do good to all men." Love, cherish and value them genuinely and sincerely. Whatever does not promote and exalt love is not godly and God-like, be it prophecy, sermon etc. If they make someone begin to see a fellow human being as their enemy, they are satanic.

> *"Fasting does not change God, it changes you ..."*

God is love and vice versa. Where there is no love, there is no God. Love sacrifices and serves. An act of service is a powerful love language or expression. It does not always want to be served but to serve. It does not envy; neither does it think evil of another person. It is not self-centred.

The only enemy we have is Satan. We are not to wrestle against flesh and blood, i.e. human beings are not your enemies. Though they are used by the devil, they are not the devil. It is the devil you need to rebuke, not the people. I love the way Apostle Paul dealt with that spirit of divination of fortune-telling using that lady in Acts 16:16-18. The most remarkable portion of the Scripture (v. 18) reads: ***"but Paul greatly annoyed, turned and said to the spirit (not the lady), I command you in the name of Jesus Christ to come out of her (the lady)."***

One other critical thing I want you to see about love is giving. There is no how you love genuinely that you will not give. The Corinthian church was commended by Paul for giving out of their poverty. That was outrageous. God is love and He gives to us liberally. However, giving is not loving, that is, not everyone who gives loves. Every lover is a giver, but not every giver is a lover. Apostle Paul's words in 1 Corinthians 13:3 enraptures my spirit: ***"And though I bestow all my goods to feed the poor, and though I give my body to be burnt, but have not love, it profits me nothing."***

Also, in 1 Corinthians 13, he stated that everything that he mentioned as what love can and cannot do and cannot do are the things God can and cannot do. This establishes the truth that God is love. If you are truly of God, you must have the capacity to love.

Anytime I preach the Word of God from 1 Corinthians 13, I encourage the congregation to see this truth by instructing them to read from verse 2 through verse 8, substituting anywhere they see "love" with "God." We can try it out here, can't we?

"2And though I bestow all my goods to feed the poor, 3and though I give my body to be burned but have not "God" it profits me nothing, 4"God" suffers long and is kind, "God" does not envy, "God" does not parade itself, is not puffed of, 5"God" does not behave rudely, "God" does not seek his own, "God" is not provoked, "God" thinks no evil, 6"God" does not rejoice in iniquity but rejoices in the truth, 7God bears all things, God believes all things, God hopes all things, "God" endures all things, 8"God" never fails".

Are the foregoing statements true or not? They are true because they reveal to us that God is love and vice versa. To be godly is to be lovely. Faith, which is founded by love, is pleasing to God. The Bible says that without faith, it is impossible to please God; and that faith is empowered and works through love. You cannot be praying without loving. Praying without loving is akin to barking. Even Jesus told us to reconcile with anybody we have issues with before going to the altar to make a sacrifice (which symbolises praying to God). You should not pretend that you have nothing against anybody. You'd better settle it first before anything else. People even love to fast, thinking that their fasting will make God do something or maybe God will pity them and grant their desire in time. The truth is, God does not respond to crocodile's tears and wailings. He responds to faith only. Anywhere He sees faith powered by love, He channels His power in that direction.

Fasting does not change God. It changes you. There is a change process that we undergo during fasting, Isaiah's account of God redefining fasting for the children of Israel in Isaiah 58 comes in handy here. The way people get it wrong now was the same thing that happened to them then. It is appalling that we keep repeating the same mistake the people of the Bible times made. Different scriptural accounts of these characters are given for our learning, correction and improvement. The Message Translation of Isaiah 58:2-9 says, **"2They ask me, 'What's the right thing to do?' and love having me on their side. 3But they also complain, 'Why do we fast and you don't look our way? Why do we humble ourselves and you don't even notice?' 'Well, here's why: 'The bottom line on your 'fast days' is profit. You drive your employees much** *too hard. ⁴You fast, but at the same time you bicker and fight. You fast, but you swing a mean fist. The kind of fasting you do won't get your prayers off the ground. ⁵Do you think this is the kind of fast day I'm after: a day to show off humility? To put on a pious long face and parade around solemnly in black? Do you call that fasting, a fast day that I, God, would like? ⁶ 'This is the kind of fast day I'm after: to break the chains of injustice, get rid of exploitation in the workplace, free the oppressed, cancel debts. ⁷What I'm interested in seeing you do is sharing your food with the hungry, inviting the homeless poor into your homes, putting clothes on the shivering ill-clad, being available to your own family. ⁸Do this and the lights will turn on, and your lives will turn around at once. Your righteousness will pave your way. The God of glory will secure your passage. ⁹Then when you pray, God will answer, You'll call out for help and I'll say, 'Here I am.'"*

Judging from the foregoing Scriptures, you can see that a life of fasting is a life of love, that is, a way of expressing love to other fellow human beings.

Pastor Kenneth E Hagin (of blessed memory), in his book –"Commonsense Guide to Fasting", narrated how used to fast for some days in the week like the Jews, but was told by God to stop acting like that and start living a fasting life. I believe the fasting life God instructed him to live was not of abstaining from food every day of his life (living without eating), but to lead a love life. Fasting without loving is akin to hunger strike. Love gives and forgives. You should live our lives walking in love. That is the fasting God wants. You should not keep malice with people. You should not be angry unreasonably. Though it is emotional, do not let it stay with you for long. Vent it out. Do not be bitter about other people's progress. Do not act towards people wickedly. Set them free. Let them give sacrificially. God-kind of love is sacrificial. Jesus sacrificed his life because He loved us. He got resurrected through the power of love. Apostle James succinctly defined a good religion as ***visit orphans and widows in their trouble, and to keep oneself unspotted from the world" (James 1:27).*** You can do it because God's love capacity has been shed abroad in your hearts by the Holy Spirit at new birth. "Do good to all men" and "never be weary in well doing for you will reap it when you do not faint" were the words of Apostle Paul in one of his epistles.

Loving people, solving their problems and meeting their needs are important if you want to have a lasting success. This is because God replicate for you what you make happen for others. Over the years, I have observed that in the process of solving people's problems, one's problem get solved, too. I have learnt not to be selfish; not to be always after my well-being only. To get scale heights at the workplace as a good team player, Richard Templar suggested in his book "The Rules of Work" to always use the word "we" in presentations, not "I." When you help others to succeed, you will not remain on the floor. Love will lift you up.

12

The Rule of Evaluation and Review

"Examine yourselves as to whether you are still in the faith. Test yourselves. Do you not know yourself...?"

- 2 Corinthians 13:5

Success without evaluation is on the brink of frustration. There should be measures in place for checks, assessments and appraisals as we journey on in life. Evaluation is key to excellence. It is evaluation that gives birth to continuous improvement, that is, continuous evaluation and review lead to continuous improvement. It is when you review your system(s) that you will know areas that need improvement. This will help you to generate action plan for correction. Areas where you are doing well will also be identified as you make plans for improvement.

I found this ERRC Grid in a book "Blue Ocean Strategy" by W. Chan Kim and Renee Mauborgne a good and applicable principle and tool for operation reviews to achieve operational excellence on a daily, weekly, monthly, bimonthly, quarterly, biannual, or annual basis. ERRC is an acronym that stands for Eliminate, Raise, Reduce and Create.

Eliminate (None of This) 1. 2. 3. 4.	**Reduce** (Less of This) 1. 2. 3. 4
Raise (More of This) 1. 2. 3. 4.	**Create** (Start This) 1. 2. 3. 4.

As you sit down to assess your performance, you need to ask yourself sincere questions bordering on your finance, marriage, spiritual, career, business, ministry etc. What are the things to be ELIMINATED? What are the things that do not add any value to your life, despite all your efforts to make productive? Jesus was not liberal with the fig tree. Once he discovered that it was not bearing fruit, He cursed it. There was no point in praying before it be productive.

"Evaluation is key to excellence" When organizations with brands, products and varying services are not giving desired results, an RCA (Root Cause Analysis) can be done. This is carried out to ascertain the outcome of the analysis and the possibility of eliminating the brand, product or service which is unproductive, despite the efforts of the company to make it work. However, if the brand you are planning to eliminate is the critical component or aspect of your business, life or ministry, please make sure you are fully convinced after praying and researching. You may be asked by God not to give up on it, although it is common sense to do away with anything that is not working.

The next step is RAISE. This focuses what to improve. When our ministry was much younger, there was one of our special meetings that was doing very well but which we saw an opportunity to improve on. With the meeting crucial to our mission, we had to brainstorm what could be done to improve its reach and awareness as well as output: getting blessed through the programme. We resorted to investing more in the programme. You can apply the same principle in your line of business as well.

REDUCE is another crucial point in operation review. Though it is important, it is not compulsory. For example, you have some calls that are important but are not compulsory to make. You do not consider them when you are trying to reduce your call costs, though you cannot delete the numbers from your phone. You choose to ignore them. Though it is drastic, it is still reduction, not elimination.

CREATE comes with innovation, thinking about new things that have never been done before but have a massive positive impact on the operation. A church pastoral team can do operation review after a Sunday service using this tool to check what are the things identified in the service that must not occur again. Such things should go into the ELIMINATE box, while things that happened and need to be improved on should go to RAISE box. Things that happened but should be minimised in subsequent services should go to REDUCE box. Things that come to our mind as creative and innovative ideas that can add value to the service should go to CREATE box. You can use this to do operation review of your family activities.

When I was in the university, a friend told me that, while reviewing their family activities on the 2nd of January of a particular year, they discovered that they had to make a drastic reduction of the phone calls they made aggregately. After making that decision, they bought a small car from the money saved by the December of that particular year. In your multi-product and multi-service business, you can apply this ERRC principle to prioritise where you channel your resources into or invest them in.

13

The G-Factor

The G-Factor is the greatest factor: it is the God Factor. Jesus, while speaking in John 15:5, said: ***"...for without Me you can do nothing."*** What a powerful statement! There is nothing we can do without God. Outside God, we are nothing.

Proverbs 21:31
"The horse is prepared for the day of battle but safety is of the Lord."

Proverbs 16:25
"There is a way that seems right to a man but the end of his death." -

Jeremiah 9:23-24

"23Thus says the Lord, let not the wise man glory in his wisdom, let's not the mighty glory in this might, not let the rich man glory in his riches, 24but let him who glories glory in this, that he understands and knows Me, that I am the Lord, exercising loving-kindness, judgment and righteousness in the earth, if for in these I delight says the Lord." Jeremiah 10:23

"O Lord, I know the way of man is not in himself; it's not in man who walks to direct his own steps."

Proverbs 3:5-7

"5Trust in the Lord with all your heart and lean not on your own understanding, 6in all your ways acknowledge Him and He will direct your paths, 7do not be wise in your own eyes."

Psalms 37:4-5

"4Delight yourself also in the Lord and He shall give you the desires of your heart. 5Commit your way to the Lord, trust also in Him and He will bring it to pass."

1 Corinthians 3:6-7 (Literal Translation)

"6I planted, Apollos watered, but God made it to grow, 7so as neither he planting is anything nor

he watering, but God making to grow." James 1:17

"Every good gift and every perfect gift is from above and comes from the Father of lights, with whom is no variableness, neither shadow of turning." -

Psalm 75:6-7

"For exaltation comes neither from the East, nor from the West, nor from the South but God is the Judge: [7]He puts down one and exalts another."

John 3:27

"A man can receive nothing except it be given him from above."

Proverbs 19:21

"There are many devices in a man's heart, but only the counsel of God shall stand." -

Psalm 127:1

"Unless the Lord builds the house, they labour in vain who build it, unless the Lord guards the city, the watchman stays awake in vain."

Dear Esteemed Reader, without God, lasting success is not in sight. As the Creator of the heaven and the earth, He owns all things. He is the only one you can run to for lasting success. As our Manufacturer, He knows every detail about our design and the exact purpose for that design. That is why the psalmist, under the powerful influence of the Holy Spirit, said, ***"Know that the Lord, He is God; It is He who has made us and not we ourselves..." (Psalm 100:3).***

> *"Without God, lasting success is not in view"*

God is the Author of our destinies. He is the One who can lead our lives into lasting success. The earlier we decide and make God our Number 1 ally, the better for us. No matter how hard we try, it is His blessings that makes rich. His principles do not have respect for any person, likewise His blessings. He does not look at people's face, age, tribe and nationality before He blesses them. As nations of the world accommodate poor people, so do they blessed people who align themselves with God and His principles. He honours His Word (principles) more than His name. Your knowledge and deed, without the G-factor, do not guarantee success.

Dear Reader, do not be frustrated by your unproductiveness. The missing link is the God-factor. Let Him be in your process from start to finish. Again, without Him, you can do nothing. He is the One to guide, lead and teach you how to prosper. He is always ready to do that for you, no matter the number of times you go to Him in prayer and through the help of the Holy Spirit.

Psalm 22: 8 says, ***"I (God) will instruct you and teach you in the way you should go; I will guide you with my eye."*** You may know all the principles of success. The truth is, you cannot apply all the principles at once. It is wisdom of God that guides you in applying a principle that is apt to a situation. Isaiah 28:24-29 establishes this point: ***"[24]Does the plow man keep plowing all day to sow? Does he keep turning his soil and breaking the clods? [25]When he has levelled its surface, does he not sow the black cummin and scatter the cummin, plant the wheat in rows, the barley in the appointed place, and the spelt in its place? [26]For He instructs him in right judgement, His God teaches him. [27]For the black Cummins is not threshed with a threshing sledge, nor is cartwheels rolled over the cummin; but the black cummin is beaten out with a stick and the cummin with a rod. [28]Bread flour must be ground; therefore he does not thresh it forever, break it with his cartwheel or crush it with his horsemen. [29]This also comes from the Lord of hosts, who is wonderful in counsel and excellent in guidance"***.

Wow! You can see that the Scriptures above explain how God can guide you in detail how to accomplish a task with respect to appropriate tools and techniques. God is ready to give you, tell you and show you patterns, templates, models and blueprints for your success in life, your now and your future. All He wants you to do is to yield to Him. Stop racking your brain to figure it out! Be simple and meek. He wants to guide you in the journey of your life. He is the Master Planner and the Extraordinary Strategist. He knows you more than you know yourself. He formed you before you were conceived.

Psalm 139:2 expounds this subject when it says, ***"You know my sitting down and my rising up; You understand my thoughts afar off, You comprehend my path and my lying down and acquainted with all my ways, for there is not a word on my tongue, but behold, O Lord, behind and before and laid Your hand upon me."*** Verse 13 says, ***"For You found my inward parts; You covered me in my mother's womb."*** Verse 16 concludes it, saying, ***"Your eyes saw my substance being yet unformed, and in Your book they all were written..."***

God is very real. He is more real than your friend or your spouse. He is the number one person in your life. Allow him to teach you. Do not be stiff-necked. Build a sweet and strong personal relationship with Him. Make receiving first-hand instructions from God a habit. When they come from another person, they should be a confirmation. Do not make gods out of the people through whom the instructions are received. You are not a bastard. Strengthen your relationship with your Father. Let communication be between you and Him.

One of my mentors told me how frustrating life was for him. After being disappointed and mocked by relations when he was at his wits' end, he told God that whatever happened afterwards should be between him and God. Since then, his path has been shining brighter.

Bishop Oyedepo always shares one of his interesting experiences with God. In this encounter, God asked to know the number of eyes he had. "Two," he said, Again, God asked whether he could look up with one and look with the other. "No," he responded. Then God told him that he should never pretend to be looking up to Him when he was actually looking up to man. Right there, he vowed that he would not struggle for what God could not give him; neither would he struggle to get to where God was not taking Him. What a profound statement! Psalm 118:8-9 says," *8It is better to trust in the Lord than*

to put confidence in man. [9]It is better to trust in the Lord than to put confidence in princes."

14

Altitude Is Attitude

It is a common saying that your attitude determines your altitude. There is a skill set to go up, while there is another skill set to stay up, likewise attitude. Let me share some of the attitudes of great men I have closely watched and learnt from.

1. Gratitude

The word "gratitude" is a portmanteau (combination) of gratefulness and attitude. Only the grateful people are great and vice versa. Learn to always say "Thank you" to God and fellow human being. Appreciate God for who He is and what He has done. Appreciate people for who they are and what they have done, too.

The Psalmist said, ***"It is good to give thanks"*** (Psalm 92:1). Only people who are thankful get their tanks full. Only those who appreciate can appreciate in value. Too many people love criticising, grumbling and complaining. They never see anything that is right about people, places and events. They are always negative. They are difficult to be impressed. Even if you see anything wrong in what someone has done or is doing, deploy sandwich communication style in reviewing it: positive (commendation), negative (constructive criticism) and positive (commendation). Never leave people with negative emotions. It is very bad. Constructive criticism is to appreciate, criticise and appreciate. It should be two appreciation statements for every one statement of criticism. Bitter pills are sometimes sugar-coated or attractively colour-coated to appeal to whoever wants to take it, not to scare or discourage the person. Feedback is a gift that can be better packaged.

"There's a skill set to go up but there is another skill set to stay up..."

Some organisations, groups and churches organise end of the year events not only for wining and dining but also for appreciating those who have contributed significantly to the growth of the system or church ministries. Organise pastors' appreciation service and workers' appreciation service. You cannot do that for someone and expect them to underperform the following year. Rather, they will exceed your targets and the previous year's baseline, knowing full well that rewards await them. That is called Motivation and Reward Theory in Management.

Once, I attended a pastor friend's birthday party organised by his members. It was elaborate. In the course of celebration, they showered him with praises and confirmed how they were aware of his prayer for them in the middle of the night; how he studied to teach them and how he used to go out of his financial budget to help some of them and many other things they said he did. Some of them were literally shedding tears while paying him tribute. A week after that event, he told me that was his appreciation service and that he had been spurred to do much more. Naturally, that is what happens after appreciation.

2. I-Am-Sorry Attitude

Many people are too arrogant and big to make this statement. They prefer playing the blame game (passing a blame to other people) to accepting responsibilities for something that goes wrong. Dear Esteemed Reader, quit the blame game, fault-finding and finger-pointing. There is no excuse for failure. Nobody's action or inaction is an excuse for your failure. The inability to own up to a fault on one's part has ruined many relationships (either with God or human). Many husbands are too big to apologise to their wives. Wives, also, are not submissive. Fathers do not say sorry to their children when they fail to fulfil a promise. Bosses do not say sorry to their subordinates. Business people do not say sorry to their customers. Pastors do not say sorry to their church members. We go on and on, wounding hearts and hurting ourselves. Apologising and accepting apology heal relationships and enliven dead ones. Never be too big to apologise and own up to your fault. Only God is perfect. We are all vulnerable to mistakes. When people sin, especially believers, they pretend that all is right and run away from God. However, there is a provision for their forgiveness in Christ, since it is not habitual and wilful. No wonder 1 John 1:8-10 says, **"8If we say that we have no sin, we deceive ourselves and the truth is not in us. 9If we confess our sins, He is faithful and just to forgive us our sins and to cleanse us from all unrighteousness. 10If we say that we have not sinned, we make Him a liar and His word is not in us."**

Apparently, this Scripture continues in the succeeding Chapter 2, like other chapters of books in the Bible. Originally, their scrolls had no divisions: chapters and verses. They were like that until they were technically and professionally arranged for reference. 1 John 2:1-2 says, **"***¹My little children, these things I write to you so that you may not sin and if anyone sins, we have an Advocate with the Father, Jesus Christ the righteous ²and He himself is the propitiation for our sins and not for ours only, but also for the whole world."** So, you should own up to your mistake and apologise.

3. Please-Help-Me Attitude

It takes humility to ask for help. Pride kills people prematurely. If you do not want to be overburdened or fatigued and if you want to enjoy excellence in all that you do, you need to learn how to ask for help. It is not a sign of weakness. Rather, it helps you to focus on what is important to you.

Many people wait until everything gets out of hand before they ask for helping hands. You are not the Almighty El-Shaddai. You will always need some help. God expects us to open up to Him for His help at any point in time. Behind every man's end is God's beginning. You need someone to meet some particular needs in your life. As a business person, you need to stop doing IT, hiring, sales, marketing, advertisement etc. by yourself and give attention to major things. Do not major on minor and vice versa. Do apply the Pareto Prioritization Principle (PPP) of focusing 80% of your time, resources and energy on the top 20% of your task that will give you 80% results. A law of success that states that the higher you go or rise, the lesser you know and focus on."

This please-help-me attitude is one of the reasons for outsourcing. Try to delegate your authority and responsibilities. You cannot do it all alone. There is no point in deceiving and killing yourself prematurely. It is not job abandonment but for effectiveness and efficiency. That is why the apostles voiced in the Book of Acts of the Apostles Chapter 6, saying: ***"It is not good for them to leave" or better put."***

> *"...only those who appreciate can appreciate ..."*

It is not good for them to minor on the major of prayer and the ministry of the Word and major in serving tables. They had to advertise for the role of deaconry to help them major on minor and keep them focused on major. Thus, we have a ministry called the Ministry of Helps in the body of Christ. In 1 Corinthians 12:28, the Scripture says, ***"And God has appointed these in the church: first apostles, second prophets, third teachers, after that miracles then gift of***

healings, helps, administrators, varieties of tongues." The Ministry of Helps is the ministry of armour-bearers. They are the hands that lift the main hand for support. The word "helps" was first used in Acts of the Apostles 27:17 to mean a rope or chain used to secure and relieve a vessel or ship so as not to sink.

4. Zero-Waste Attitude

Jesus, while addressing the gathered crowd after feeding them with the multiplied five loaves of bread and two fish, said, "Gather up the remaining fragments so that nothing is lost, and they were able to gather twelve baskets." Jesus was a perfect business-oriented man. He had what I call the business mindset. Every serious-minded business individual has that thinking of waste reduction and waste elimination (also called LEAN thinking). It is a consideration of the expenditure of resources for any goal other than the creation of value for the end customer to be wasteful. Today, I see many business organisations treading this path, possibly because of the global economic challenge and many other internal issues. The essence is to remain in business; hence, I will encourage every individual and organisation to go LEAN today to grow fat tomorrow by cutting the excesses and controlling your wasteful habit.

Management is not only managing resources when limited but when they are surplus. Many people do not have capacity to manage abundance. Thus, they have not been entrusted with abundance despite their prayer. Some people's capital is in the money they waste for pleasures. Again, I challenge you to go all out against waste.

15

The God of Mercy Is the God of another Chance

One of the amazing things about the account of the mercy of God in the Bible is the story of Samson despite his mistakes which culminated in the loss of his God-given strength. Judges16:22 says, ***"But the hair of his head began to grow again."***

God's mercy endures forever. His patience is till the end of ages. God is interested in giving you another chance, as long as you are willing to rise up from where you have fallen and put on your strength, having realised your mistakes or pitfalls.

God, speaking through Prophet Joel about the restoration of last years, said, ***"And I will restore to you the years which the swarming locust has eaten, the locust larvae, and the stripping locust and the***

cutting locust, My great army which I sent among you" (Joel 2:25). I believe you can also claim this prophecy for yourself and begin to walk in the newness of year, starting with a clean state of a fresh hope, new dreams and clear-cut, divinely-inspired visions.

If you do not have a meaningful relationship with God, there is no point in trying to apply any of the rules in this book. This is because it is only His blessings that can give your life a meaning. I urge you to welcome God into the affairs of your life today as you say this prayer.

Lord Jesus, I acknowledge that I am a sinner and my sins have separated me from You, I ask that you forgive me my sins, come into my heart, and be the Lord of my life, in Jesus' Name. Amen.

If you have just said that prayer, I congratulate you and welcome you on board to a life of meaning and eternal significance. I urge you to read your Bible, pray and find a local church or assembly of believers where you can learn more about God, His Word and this life of meaning as you fellowship with other great minds. You cannot be among the giants and remain a dwarf.

I pray for you that you will fulfil destiny. I decree that your lost years will be restored; the lost times will be redeemed and you will recover all. The Lord will give you double honour for your past shames. Your struggle has ended. Your warfare is finished. I command that you walk from victory to victory; from glory to glory and from strength to strength. Amen.

If this book has been a big blessing to you and you need to make enquiries or share your praise reports with us via **odunlamiolugbenga07@gmail.com.**

Connect with me on:

www.gbengaodunlamisignatures.com